Author: Kene Elistrand

ISBN HARDBACK: 978-1-80562-819-4

ISBN PAPERBACK: 978-1-80564-340-1

Whispers of Gossamer Strands

In twilight's breath, the shadows play,
A dance of dreams in soft array.
Winds carry secrets, sweet and light,
Where stars awaken in the night.

Each whispered tale, like silver thread,
Ties heart to heart, where love is bred.
Gossamer strands that softly bind,
A tapestry of the heart and mind.

Through fields of glimmer, the fairies flit,
In moonlit smiles, their laughter lit.
A world of wonder, forever spun,
Where magic lives, and fears are none.

The trees lean in to hear the song,
Of fleeting time, where we belong.
With every breath, a wish can soar,
In whispers soft, forevermore.

Enchantment in the Dewdrop Glade

Beneath the boughs of ancient trees,
The dewdrops shimmer in the breeze.
In the glade where silence breathes,
Enchantment lingers, softly weaves.

With every step on velvet grass,
Time dances by, as moments pass.
The sun spills gold on leaves of green,
A world alive, so bright, serene.

Whispers echo in the morning light,
Where dreams take flight and hearts feel bright.
In every droplet, magic swirls,
A promise held in nature's pearls.

The laughter of fairies fills the air,
A gentle warmth, beyond compare.
In every shadow, stories stay,
In the dewdrop glade, they find their way.

Dreams Woven with Moonlight

In the stillness of the night,
Dreams are woven, pure and bright.
Threads of silver, soft and thin,
Casting spells where dreams begin.

Moonlight dances on whispering waves,
A lullaby that gently saves.
With every breath, a story stirs,
In the silence, the heart confers.

Stars like lanterns in a sea of dark,
Dreams set sail, their guiding spark.
In twilight's embrace, hope takes flight,
Through realms unseen, in endless night.

I close my eyes, the journey starts,
To lands where magic fills the hearts.
With every soft and sighing breath,
I find my peace, I conquer death.

Secrets Veiled in Petal Softness

In gardens where the roses bloom,
Secrets linger, dispelling gloom.
Their petals soft, with whispers sweet,
Embrace the sun where shadows meet.

Each colour tells a tale untold,
Of love and laughter, brave and bold.
In fragrant air, in gentle sway,
Petals carry dreams away.

Beneath the moon's soft, silver gaze,
Beauty flourishes in hidden ways.
In every bud, a story lies,
Waiting for dawn to recognize.

Secrets veiled in morning dew,
Awakening hearts, forever new.
With every bloom, a wish set free,
In gardens vast, for you and me.

Willow Wreathed Tales of Enchantment

In a glade where whispers dwell,
The willows weave their magic spell.
With branches low and shadows deep,
They cradle secrets, dreamers keep.

Underneath their emerald lace,
Lost stories find their resting place.
Where moonlight filters through the green,
A thousand wonders still unseen.

The rustle of the leaves in flight,
Sings softly to the starry night.
From ancient roots, new tales arise,
Awakening the sleepy skies.

In every twist, a legend spun,
Of battles fought and victories won.
The river's song, a gentle guide,
To every heart where dreams abide.

So wander near the willow's shade,
Where every soul can be remade.
In tales that dance through time and space,
The magic lives in every trace.

Fae's Veil Dance in the Emerald Grove

In the heart of emerald trees,
Fae folk waltz on whispered breeze.
Their laughter twirls with morning's light,
In shadows deep, out of our sight.

With wings that shimmer, softly gleam,
They pull us into nature's dream.
In every step, a spell unfolds,
As ancient magic gently molds.

Beneath the boughs where glimmers play,
The fae's enchantments lead the way.
With every twirl, a tale takes flight,
Of love eternal, pure delight.

In twilight's blush, their dance awakens,
A symphony of hearts unshaken.
Through the grove, they flit and dart,
Kindling wonder in each heart.

So let the moon guide you to roam,
In this enchanted, secret home.
Where fae and nature swirl and blend,
A dancing veil that has no end.

Ethereal Graces of Glistening Hair

Upon the winds, her tresses flow,
Like liquid gold in soft moon glow.
Each strand a story, rich and rare,
A whispered charm, a fragrant air.

With gentle hands, she braids the light,
Into her hair, pure dreams take flight.
A shimmering waterfall cascades,
In every curl, a magic fades.

The stars would envy such a hue,
In midnight's grasp, a shade so true.
Her hair a realm where wishes dwell,
A timeless spell, a silken well.

As dawn approaches, colors shift,
Ethereal grace begins to lift.
In every wave, the universe,
Reveals the truths that hearts immerse.

So wander close, and drink it in,
The beauty woven deep within.
In glistening locks, the heavens share,
A tapestry beyond compare.

Whispered Secrets of Mystical Locks

In chambers closed where shadows play,
Mystical locks keep doubts at bay.
With secret knots and patterns spun,
Unraveled tales of hearts begun.

Each twist and turn, a story lives,
Of strength and love that fate gives.
Silken strands in moonlit air,
Hold whispered secrets, soft and rare.

The veil of night embraces soft,
These hidden truths that float aloft.
In every braid, a wish concealed,
A promise made, a fate revealed.

So listen close, and feel the pull,
Of every story, every lull.
These mystical locks embrace the night,
With every breath, release the light.

For in each curl, a promise dwells,
Of journeys taken, of ringing bells.
In whispered secrets time forgot,
The magic lies in every knot.

The Twisted Weave of Nature's Secret

In emerald whispers, secrets dwell,
A tapestry where dreams compel.
The twilight hums a mystic tune,
While shadows dance beneath the moon.

Roots entwined in echoes old,
Stories of the brave and bold.
In every rustle, magic sings,
Unveiling what the silence brings.

Underneath the ancient oaks,
Nature weaves her gentle strokes.
With woven branches, thoughts entwine,
In secret glades, the worlds align.

Lush Manes in Celestial Gardens

In gardens rich with colors bright,
Where flowers bask in morning light.
There prance the steeds of dreams untold,
With flowing manes of silk and gold.

Each petal glistens, soft and fair,
As whispers drift upon the air.
In laughter woven through the leaves,
A symphony the heart believes.

With every grace, they dance and play,
Beneath the sun's warm, golden ray.
In timeless spins of joy and mirth,
They herald wonders of the earth.

Glistening Filaments of Wonder

Beneath the stars, the threads take flight,
In luminous webs spun soft and bright.
Each filament a tale to weave,
Of hopes and dreams that we conceive.

The night unfolds with whispers low,
A secret path where dreams can flow.
Through twilight's grasp, the visions gleam,
And light the shadows with a dream.

In silken strands, the magic sways,
Reflecting all the wondrous ways.
The universe in each soft glow,
A tapestry of joy to sow.

The Serpent's Caress on Sylvan Skin

In woodland depths where silence reigns,
A serpent glides through quiet lanes.
With scales that shimmer, dark and bright,
It dances softly in the night.

Its graceful form, a whispered sigh,
A fleeting flash that slips on by.
With every coil, the shadows weave,
A mystery the dawn won't leave.

Upon the skin of nature's weave,
The serpent's charm, a magic reprieve.
In silence held, the secrets spin,
A tale of life that lives within.

Twists of Enchantment in Nature's Lap

In the glade where shadows play,
Whispers dance on breezes light.
Mossy carpets softly sway,
Painting dreams in shades of night.

Twilight's veil begins to fall,
Stars awake in quiet gleam.
Crickets chirp their evening call,
Nature wrapped in silver dream.

Through the thickets, secrets flow,
Flowery scents in the night air.
Hidden wonders, ebb and flow,
Magic twinkles everywhere.

Gentle streams like lullabies,
Sparkling under moonlit skies.
Each rustle beneath the trees,
Sings of joy and mysteries.

So let wanderers find their way,
In this realm where wonders nap.
Embrace the magic of the day,
In enchantments' sweet, soft lap.

Where Fae Secrets Twine

In the thicket, soft and bright,
Fae whisper secrets, old and wise.
Glimmering wands, a twinkling sight,
Peeking through stars, like fireflies.

Under moonbeams' silver glow,
Dancing shadows spin and sway.
Mysteries in hearts do grow,
As fae weave night into day.

Listen closely to the breeze,
Every rustle hides a tale.
Magic hides within the trees,
In every whispered, gentle wail.

Petal soft, where dreams collide,
Nature's rhythm sings in time.
Join the dance where shadows bide,
In this fae-born world, sublime.

So wander deep, let spirits guide,
Through the glen where fairies twine.
With each step, the veil's beside,
Fae secrets weave, in love divine.

Lullabies Woven in Ethereal Locks

In the quiet of the night,
Cradled by a silver beam,
Softly weaving dreams in flight,
Woven whispers, tender seam.

Hushed the world, the stars awake,
Brushing against the velvet sky.
Lullabies of hearts they make,
From the echoes of a sigh.

Tresses flowing like the streams,
Captured in the moon's embrace.
Woven tales of hopes and dreams,
Twinkling on each starry face.

Gentle hands of night do weave,
Murmuring comforting spells.
In the depths of hearts believe,
Ethereal locks, secret wells.

So close your eyes and drift away,
In the cradle of the night.
Let those woven dreams hold sway,
As magic glows in cloistered light.

Graceful Shadows in the Garden of Light

In the garden, where shadows dance,
Beneath the blooms, the sunbeams play.
Graceful forms, they dart and prance,
Life's sweet symphony in a ballet.

Petals whisper with the breeze,
Colors burst in joyful cheer.
Nature's art, the heart it frees,
With every bloom, springtime near.

On gentle paths, where footsteps tread,
Sunlight filters through the green.
Where the secrets bloom and spread,
In each corner, magic's seen.

So linger long, let senses soar,
In this garden, pure delight.
Here, every shadow speaks of yore,
Whispers of a world so bright.

Nature's grace, forever twined,
In every heart, her beauty shines.
Through graceful shadows, secrets find,
In gardens' light, where love aligns.

Flickers of Twilight Tresses

In the hush where shadows dwell,
Flickers dance like whispered spells.
Tresses weave through twilight's hue,
Caressing dreams that feel so true.

Stars arise as shadows sigh,
Glimmers fade but never die.
Each lock a tale of night's embrace,
Twilight's kiss on every face.

Winds of fate with gentle grace,
Pull us close to this sacred place.
Where time stands still, and hearts take flight,
In the soft glow of fading light.

Laughter of the Woodland Spirits

In the glades where laughter rings,
Woodland spirits weave their flings.
Joyful echoes in the air,
Mysteries lurking everywhere.

With tiny feet they dance and play,
Guiding lost souls on their way.
Through leafy boughs their giggles flow,
A charming tune, a sweet tableau.

They whisper secrets to the trees,
Invite the winds, enchant the bees.
In twilight's glow, pure magic stirs,
Each moment wrapped in gentle purrs.

Lush Locks Beneath Star-Kissed Skies

Beneath the sky where starlights gleam,
Lush locks spill like a silken dream.
Whispers float on the softer breeze,
Entwined with grace, we feel at ease.

With every flicker, every light,
Our souls ignite in the quiet night.
Each twinkling star a knot of fate,
Binding hearts that love relate.

In shadows deep, we find the glow,
Of memories past and hopes that flow.
A tapestry rich, woven tight,
Lush locks dance in the moon's delight.

Fragrant Breezes and Shimmering Threads

In fragrant breezes, whispers glide,
Through shimmering threads of dreams that bide.
Each scent a tale, each sigh a song,
Carried forth where we all belong.

Through colorful hues, the fabrics weave,
Stories of hearts that dare believe.
With every touch, a world unfolds,
In delicate shades of crimson and gold.

As twilight falls, the echoes call,
Inviting us to where nightfall enthralls.
With threads of magic, we gently sew,
A tapestry rich with love's soft glow.

Winding Whispers of the Air

In the hush of dreams where shadows play,
Soft secrets ride on wings of gray.
The rustling leaves tell tales untold,
In whispers low, the night unfolds.

Breezes carry fragments of the past,
Notes of laughter, gentle and vast.
Through branches swaying, stories glide,
In every gust, where memories bide.

With each flutter, a heartbeat shared,
The air weaves magic, brilliant and rare.
Moments linger in fragrant sighs,
As starlight bathes the midnight skies.

In corridors of time, they drift and sway,
Like spirits charting a silvered way.
Each breath a bond, so delicately spun,
Whispers of air, till the night is done.

A tapestry of echoes soft and clear,
In every corner, love draws near.
For in these whispers, though fleeting and small,
Lies the enchantment that binds us all.

Glorious Cascades in Nature's Embrace

In mountain's cradle, waters flow,
A dance of droplets, a sparkling show.
Sunlight kisses the shimmering stream,
While nature hums a gentle dream.

Rushing whispers over stones they glide,
In joyous laughter, they cascade wide.
With every splash, the world awakes,
In shimmering veil, the river shakes.

Beneath the ferns, in shadows deep,
Nature's wonders, a secret to keep.
Each curve and bend, with grace it wanders,
In glades adorned, where beauty ponders.

The song of water, wild and free,
Sings of life's sweet harmony.
A tranquil heart, in rhythm's flow,
In nature's arms, our spirits grow.

A tapestry woven with emerald hue,
In glorious splendor, the world anew.
For in these cascades, our troubles cease,
In nature's embrace, we find our peace.

The Starlit Weave of Illusions

In the canvas night where dreams entwine,
Stars flicker softly, a dance divine.
From the depths of dark, where visions play,
Illusions shimmer, leading hearts astray.

Veils of light in the midnight air,
Whispered secrets linger everywhere.
Threads of hopes, in silver spun,
Weaving tales of what's begun.

The cosmos sways with a timeless grace,
Where fantasies dwell in outer space.
Each twinkling gem, a promise bright,
In the tapestry of endless night.

As gentle winds carry wishes far,
Beneath the glow of a wishing star.
In dreams, we linger, in shadows roam,
While starlit secrets beckon us home.

A dance of spirits, woven tight,
In the heart of darkness, we seek the light.
For in this weave, both fragile and bold,
Lies the magic of stories yet to be told.

Traces of Twilight in Glistening Locks

As twilight drapes the world in gold,
Glistening strands of stories unfold.
With whispered breezes that trace the night,
In every lock, a spark of light.

The hues of dusk blend soft and warm,
A gentle embrace, a tender form.
In every shimmer, a memory clings,
As twilight dances, our spirit sings.

With every heartbeat, the shadows blend,
In the hush of night, we twist and bend.
Each strand a journey, a tale to share,
In glistening locks, the world laid bare.

The mirror of time, as it softly glows,
Reflects the moments that life bestows.
Through tangled threads and silken strands,
Twilight whispers from distant lands.

In every flicker, a memory stays,
As night unfolds in a myriad of ways.
For in these locks, the universe spins,
A testament to where our story begins.

Ethereal Threads of Dreams

In twilight's hush, the whispers weave,
A tapestry of stars, believe.
With silken threads, they softly glow,
As secrets dance in moonlit flow.

Each dream a leaf on winds that sigh,
In realms where waking thoughts can fly.
The night reveals its magic's thread,
Where wishes wand and stories spread.

Upon the breeze, lost tales drift near,
Fleeting glimmers, sweet and clear.
They sway and spin, a gentle fray,
In dreamers' hearts, they softly play.

A silver mist, the echoes hum,
In worlds where shadows softly come.
A touch of starlight, a tender beam,
The fabric of our fondest dream.

So close your eyes and take the flight,
Through threads of dreams that spark the night.
With every stitch, a tale is spun,
In ethereal realms, we're never done.

Luminous Tangles in the Glade

In emerald glade where shadows dance,
The fireflies weave a shooting glance.
Among the moss, in silver light,
Luminous tangles spark the night.

With every flicker, stories bloom,
In twinkling spells that chase the gloom.
The nightingale's soft song entwined,
Lures wandering hearts, both bold and blind.

Branches sway in a gentle tease,
Whispers float on the midnight breeze.
A world alive with magic's spark,
In hidden realms where dreams embark.

Each tangle shines with hope anew,
A glimmer stretched across the blue.
In every twirl, a secret spins,
In illuminated paths, life begins.

So seek the glade where light unfurls,
In nature's arms, a dance of swirls.
With every breath the night imparts,
Luminous tangles touch our hearts.

A Dance of Gossamer Strands

In twilight air, the fairies twine,
With gossamer strands, they craft the line.
Each filament, a whispered grace,
That shimmers bright in secret space.

With every twist, the magic flows,
A waltz of light that softly glows.
They pirouette on silken breeze,
And weave their dreams with playful ease.

Among the blooms, their laughter rings,
The world alive with vibrant things.
A tapestry of joy, they spin,
In these soft threads, the tales begin.

So close your eyes and weave along,
In dreams where echoes form a song.
A dance of strands both pure and free,
In every heart, the magic be.

So let them guide you through the night,
With gossamer strands, a soft delight.
In every step, a tale unfurls,
This dance of dreams, a gift to twirls.

Fae's Breath on Gentle Waves

On moonlit shores where memories drift,
Fae's breath stirs the waves, a gentle gift.
With tender whispers, the night ignites,
As secrets sail on the ocean's sights.

In silken air, the currents weave,
A lullaby the seas believe.
Each ripple tells of tales untold,
In tides where shimmering dreams unfold.

With feathered grace, the light descends,
Among the shells, the magic bends.
A dance of light on water's crest,
In fae's embrace, we find our rest.

So close your eyes and let it flow,
The heartbeat of the sea below.
With every wave, a wish sets sail,
In fae's soft breath, we shall not fail.

For on this shore, let dreams arise,
With every whisper, the heart complies.
In gentle waves, the world aligns,
And fae's sweet breath in love entwines.

Enchanted Curls in the Fairy's Keep

In the depths where whispers twine,
Curls that glisten, soft and fine,
Fairy fingers dance with glee,
Weaving dreams for all to see.

Moonlit laughter fills the air,
Secrets hidden, joys to share,
Every loop a tale unfolds,
Of ancient magic, bright as gold.

Tangles hold the stories dear,
Woven strands of hope and cheer,
In their midst, a wish to keep,
In the fairy's garden deep.

Gossamer threads of silver hue,
Guide lost souls to something new,
With each curl, a path is spun,
Beneath the gaze of stars undone.

In twilight's glow, the fairies meet,
Spinning legends, bittersweet,
Curls enchanted, secrets kept,
In the keeper's heart, they leapt.

Threads of Legends in the Green Hollow

In the green hollow where shadows gleam,
Threads of legends weave a dream,
Each filament, a story told,
Of brave hearts and heroes bold.

Mossy paths and ivy walls,
Echoing with ancient calls,
The whispers of time entwined,
In the fabric fate designed.

Underneath the emerald veil,
A tapestry begins to sail,
With every stitch, a world awakes,
A boundless realm, where magic breaks.

Cloaked in hues of amber light,
Adventurers brave seek the night,
For in the threads of woven lore,
Lie dreams of triumphs, forever more.

In this hollow, magic sings,
With every breath, the heart takes wing,
And woven deep in every seam,
Are echoes of the wildest dream.

Reflections of Luminescent Locks

In the mirror's edge, they glow bright,
Locks of wonder, pure delight,
Luminescent strands that shine,
Whisper secrets, soft, divine.

Each reflection tells a tale,
Of potions brewed and magic sail,
Where every curl holds dreams at bay,
In twilight's dance, they softly sway.

Glimmers caught in silken threads,
Of daring quests and love that spreads,
Rippling echoes, pure and true,
In every twist, a heartfelt hue.

Capturing essence of the night,
Dressing shadows in gentle light,
Beneath the stars, they twist and turn,
As softest embers slowly burn.

In this place where time stands still,
Luminescent locks bend to will,
Bathing souls in radiant grace,
Reflections of a timeless place.

The Ballad of the Winding Strands

In the morning dew, they rise high,
Winding strands beneath the sky,
With every breeze, they dance and sway,
A melody that bids the day.

Tales of wonder, softly spun,
From glimmers caught in morning sun,
Each twist a passion, every braid,
A harmony that will not fade.

Through fields of dreams they intertwine,
Winding paths like ancient vine,
In the heart of nature's song,
The strands of time, forever strong.

When twilight whispers, softly glows,
Winding secrets in gentle flows,
A magic woven into night,
With each strand, a wish takes flight.

So raise your voice, let the world hear,
The ballad sung by those who steer,
Through winding strands, where dreams expand,
In the tapestry of this vast land.

Echoes of Faery Lullabies

In twilight gardens, whispers weave,
Dreams take flight on silvered leaves.
Stars ignite with a gentle glow,
While faery voices softly flow.

Crickets sing their hushed refrain,
As moonlit paths begin to wane.
Each melody a secret shared,
With every heart that truly cared.

The nightingale twirls in delight,
Dancing shadows, pure and light.
Beneath the boughs where magic sleeps,
The lullabies of starlight keep.

With velvet tones and soft embrace,
They beckon dreams to find their place.
A symphony of hope ascends,
Where faery magic never ends.

Tendrils of Mist in the Heart of the Grove

In the grove where silence breathes,
Morning mist with secrets weaves.
Tendrils curling, softly sway,
Guiding wanderers on their way.

The trees, they hum a tune so sweet,
As nature's rhythms pulse and beat.
With every step, the ground below,
Whispers tales of long ago.

Sunlight filters, golden kiss,
A gentle warmth, a fleeting bliss.
In shadows deep, the wildflowers bloom,
Painting hues in nature's loom.

The breeze entwines with every sound,
Awakening the world around.
In the heart where magic resides,
Tendrils of mist, our guide abides.

The Dance of Celestial Curls

In starlit skies, a twirl begins,
Painting dreams where hope transcends.
Celestial curls of silver light,
Embrace the dark, ignite the night.

With every twist, the galaxies spin,
Revealing wonders deep within.
Gravity's pull, a gentle sway,
As time and space begin to play.

The cosmos hums a vibrant song,
Where spirits dance and hearts belong.
In that embrace, we find our place,
Lost in the rhythm, a timeless chase.

Stars wink softly, a knowing gleam,
Within their dance lies every dream.
Celestial curls, in harmony blend,
Where beginnings fade and never end.

Mystic Weavings of the Elfin Night

Beneath the moon's enchanting beam,
Elfin whispers weave a dream.
Threads of silver, softly spun,
Create a tapestry, brightly run.

In twilight's grasp, the shadows creep,
Mystic secrets silently seep.
With every stitch, a tale unfolds,
In the heart of magic, where time holds.

Glowing orbs in the sky ascend,
Brightening paths where dreamers wend.
As nightingale serenades the skies,
Elfin laughter softly flies.

With twinkling lights in the boundless deep,
Enchantments linger, secrets keep.
In the fabric of night, we find delight,
In mystic weavings of the Elfin night.

Veils of Ethereal Beauty

In twilight's grasp, the shadows dance,
Beneath the moon's soft, shimmering glance.
Whispers of starlight in the air,
Veils of beauty, delicate and rare.

Fleeting moments, time stands still,
Nature's secrets, hearts to thrill.
Each petal holds a tale untold,
A world where dreams and magic unfold.

With every breath, the night unfolds,
Through murmured songs, the silence holds.
In every shadow, a story lies,
Beneath the watchful, ancient skies.

Glistening dewdrops on leaves aglow,
Soft echoes of a distant flow.
A woodland symphony plays on repeat,
In echoes timeless, soft and sweet.

Emerging dawn brings colors bright,
As dreams dissolve into the light.
Yet, in the depths of memory's sea,
Veils of beauty will always be.

The Charm of Unseen Whispers

In hidden corners, secrets rest,
Softly spoken, they wear a vest.
A gentle breeze, a call from night,
Whispers of shadows, soft and light.

Every rustle holds a tale,
In quiet moments, hearts set sail.
Echoes of laughter, distant cheer,
In every whisper, love draws near.

Stars above with twinkling eyes,
Gracing the whispers as they rise.
In the rustle of leaves, a dream,
Where mystery reigns, a silver gleam.

Draw near, and let the silence speak,
In every pause, the words you seek.
Unseen charm in the night's embrace,
Binding souls in a tender space.

In the shadows, hearts entwine,
Lost in the magic, destiny's line.
With every breath, a promise lives,
The charm of whispers, love's gifts to give.

In the Embrace of Forest Dreams

Beneath the boughs, where shadows play,
In forest dreams, we drift away.
Each rustling leaf a lullaby,
A whispered promise from the sky.

In twilight's glow, the spirits leap,
As night enfolds the world in sleep.
Forgotten paths and ancient trees,
Invite the heart to wander free.

Amidst the ferns, the fairies dance,
In moonlit glades, lost in a trance.
Every heartbeat, nature's hymn,
A symphony where dreams begin.

Crickets serenade the stars above,
As if the night is wrapped in love.
The forest breathes, a sacred space,
In its embrace, a sweet solace.

With morning's light, the dreams will fade,
Yet in our hearts, the magic stayed.
In the forest's arms, forever we roam,
Finding in dreams, a timeless home.

Velvet Night and Starlit Strands

Under velvet night, the world aglow,
Starlit strands weave tales we know.
Each twinkle sings of dreams anew,
Magic embedded in every view.

The gentle hush of evening's breath,
Wraps the earth in a cloak of rest.
Whispers of love in moonbeams cast,
Carrying wishes from the past.

With every star, a passion glows,
In the tapestry where starlight flows.
Threads of silver, a celestial dance,
Crafting dreams that dare to prance.

In shadows deep, hope's light remains,
Lifting souls through joy and pains.
The velvet night, a soft embrace,
Cradling hearts in its warm grace.

As dawn approaches, colors blend,
Yet in the night, our dreams ascend.
For in the quiet, life's wonders stay,
Velvet nights will lead the way.

The Ethereal Caress of Nature's Weave

In the woods where silence breathes,
Whispers of the leaves entwine,
Gentle secrets nature weaves,
In every shadow, every sign.

Sunlight dances on the stream,
Casting sparkles, pure and bright,
A tapestry of dreams may gleam,
In the soft embrace of light.

Mossy carpets, emerald hue,
Invite the weary soul to rest,
Where hidden creatures stir anew,
Nature's heart beats in its chest.

Petals flutter, soft and sweet,
A symphony of colors bloom,
In the rhythm of nature's beat,
Each corner sings, dispelling gloom.

As twilight cloaks the day in grey,
Stars emerge like jewels aglow,
And nature's whispers softly sway,
In the night's embrace, all flow.

Threads of Whimsy in the Forest

Beneath the arching boughs, we roam,
With laughter echoing through the trees,
Where fairy tales may call this home,
And every breeze brings gentle ease.

Mushrooms peek from leafy beds,
While sunbeams paint the forest floor,
A carpet stitched with nature's threads,
Where wonder waits at every door.

Tiny creatures' tales unfold,
In rustling leaves and skittered flight,
While stories of the brave and bold,
Whisper softly in the night.

Golden hues in twilight's glow,
As shadows stretch and dance about,
The wildflowers in a row,
Join in nature's playful shout.

With each step, a magic found,
In every nook and quiet space,
The forest hums a lively sound,
A whimsical, enchanted place.

Whirlwind of Pastels under Evening's Light

As dusk arrives, the sky ignites,
With hues of pink and softest blue,
A painter's palette, sheer delights,
Where day bids night a fond adieu.

Gentle breezes stir the air,
Carrying scents of sweet perfume,
Twilight drapes with tender care,
As shadows lengthen, softly loom.

Cards of clouds drift slowly by,
Stretched like dreams across the night,
To catch a glimpse of stars on high,
And dance beneath the moon's soft light.

Every hue a whispered sigh,
Each gradient a tender kiss,
In nature's breath, we learn to fly,
Awash in evening's serene bliss.

So let the colors swirl and blend,
In this workshop of the skies,
Where every moment starts to mend,
And time takes flight on pastel dyes.

A Symphony of Tresses in the Dusk

In tangled hair of autumn leaves,
The whispers of the wind do play,
A symphony of nature weaves,
As daylight softly fades away.

Branches bow with tired grace,
The sun dips low, a painted sky,
In every nook, a secret place,
Where echoes of the day drift by.

Murmurs rise from velvet glades,
As evening casts its gentle spell,
A melody in twilight fades,
In tunes that only time can tell.

The rustle of the night begins,
As stars peek through the darkened veil,
A song of dusk, where magic spins,
A fairy tale, an ancient tale.

So linger here where shadows dance,
And let the quiet stories flow,
In nature's arms, a sweet romance,
A symphony of dusk's soft glow.

Glimmering Veils of Nymphs

In the twilight's gentle hue,
Where the silver waters kiss,
Nymphs weave veils of light anew,
In dreams of fleeting bliss.

Their laughter rings like chimes,
Soft whispers through the trees,
In the secret world of rhymes,
A dance upon the breeze.

With petals in their hair,
They twirl in summer's glow,
Spinning stories rich and rare,
For those who dare to know.

Each shimmer tells a tale,
Of loves both lost and found,
While twilight weaves the veil,
Where magic's spun around.

So follow where they lead,
Through realms of hope and light,
For in their hearts they heed,
The call of endless night.

Ghostly Locks in the Mystic Forest

In the forest deep and dark,
Where shadows dare to creep,
Whispers echo, ghosts embark,
In secrets they must keep.

With hair like mist and moonlight,
They glide through ancient trees,
Casting spells both soft and slight,
On haunting melodies.

Each step a silent prayer,
For lovers lost in dreams,
Guided by a presence rare,
In shimmering moonbeams.

The fragrance of the night air,
Brings tales of timeless grace,
Awakening hearts laid bare,
In this enchanted place.

So wander, if you dare,
Through heartfelt shadows' play,
For in a ghost's sweet lair,
Lies magic come what may.

Melodies of Curled Whispers

Softly sung on starlit nights,
Curled whispers of the past,
Filling hearts with sweet delights,
In the glow of shadows cast.

With every tone a memory,
Of laughter lost in time,
They dance in wild reverie,
In a lilting, gentle rhyme.

Sweet serenades of dreams,
Flow like rivers deep,
In the moonlight's softest beams,
Where lovers dare to leap.

A tapestry of sound spins,
Binding hearts forever,
In the tide of twilight wins,
A bond no storm can sever.

So linger in their song's embrace,
Let the music guide your way,
For in these curls of grace,
Lies magic in the sway.

Spun Dreams in the Fae's Realm

In a realm where fairies play,
Dreams are spun on shimmering wings,
With twilight's touch, they sway,
In a dance that softly sings.

Crafting tales of joy and cheer,
With starlight in their eyes,
They whisper secrets, sweet and clear,
Beneath the velvet skies.

Every flutter, every twirl,
A promise held so dear,
In the tapestry they unfurl,
A world that draws you near.

So follow where the magic glows,
Through the paths of dreams untamed,
Where laughter's melody flows,
In dreams that can't beclaimed.

For here in the Fae's embrace,
All troubles drift away,
In a realm of boundless grace,
Where night dances into day.

Fae Locks Adrift in Starlit Breezes

In moonlit glades, the whispers sway,
Fae locks dance in soft array,
With glimmers bright from fairy tears,
They weave through dreams and chase away fears.

A breeze of magic, wild and free,
Twists through branches of the ancient tree,
Sparkling laughter fills the air,
As night ignites with twinkling flare.

Beneath the stars, where shadows play,
The night unravels in sweet ballet,
With every flicker, stories unfold,
Of secrets kept and wonders bold.

A symphony of ethereal sighs,
Comes woven through deep velvet skies,
The fae lend grace to nature's song,
Where all belong, where all are strong.

In twilight's breath, enchantments hum,
On love's soft wings, in blessings come,
For in the heart of night's embrace,
The fae locks twirl in timeless grace.

Enchantment Woven in Crispy Dews

With dawn's first light, the leaves do gleam,
In crispy dews, enchantments dream,
Cobbled paths of glistening hue,
Awake the world with whispers new.

From petal's crown to serpent's night,
Nature's magic dances in delight,
Each droplet holds a tale untold,
Of love and warmth in morning's fold.

Beneath the arches of blooming cheer,
The shivers of summer gently near,
A tapestry of colors bright,
In dews, the dawn takes joyful flight.

Veils of fog, they rise and sway,
In harmony with the break of day,
Crisp air wraps around like a song,
Where souls find solace and belong.

Through whispered leaves and shimmering dew,
The heart of nature bids adieu,
Yet, in its dance, a promise lay,
Of enchantment's return in bright array.

Threads of the Night's Heart

In velvet shadows, time stands still,
Threads of the night weave dreams to fill,
With whispers warm as silken lace,
Each moment a touch of twilight's grace.

The stars align, a cosmic thread,
Linking wishes softly tread,
With every heartbeat, the universe spins,
Drawing closer the stories within.

A sigh of breezes, soft and light,
Carries secrets through endless night,
The heart of time, a gentle guide,
In starlit realms, where shadows abide.

Within the dark, a doorway unlocked,
To where the dreams of spirits flocked,
Each glimmer a tapestry unspun,
Embraced by the dance, forever one.

For in the weave of night's embrace,
The threads entwined find their place,
In harmony with the moon's soft art,
Whispers linger in the night's heart.

A Caress of Shadows and Light

In twilight's glow, shadows awaken,
With a caress, the silence taken,
Where flickers of hope begin to stream,
Lost in the weave of a fragile dream.

Soft whispers float, a gentle sigh,
Dancing beneath the cobalt sky,
With every flicker, a breath of night,
Merging shadows with the dawn's light.

The dance of dusk, a graceful fall,
Calls to the night, enthralling call,
Where echoes linger, secrets curl,
In twilight's arms, two worlds unfurl.

A tapestry of softest hues,
Blessing the world in radiant views,
For shadows know, and light reveals,
A sacred truth that the heart feels.

So let the night weave tales of old,
In whispers sweet and spirits bold,
For in the caress of shadowy flight,
We find our peace, our love, our light.

Shimmering Threads of the Enchanted Realm

In twilight's glow, where shadows dance,
The threads of magic weave and prance.
With every whisper of the night,
The universe ignites with light.

Beneath the stars, the faeries spin,
Their laughter echoes, soft, like din.
In gardens lush, and dreams unfurled,
They stitch the seams of this vast world.

A gentle breeze, a spark of fate,
Entwining hearts, they celebrate.
In hallowed woods where secrets creep,
The shimmering threads entwine and leap.

Ascend the hills, through misty skies,
Where ancient woodlands hush their sighs.
The path ahead with wonder glows,
As shimmering threads guide where it flows.

So step with faith, let spirits guide,
In realms where magic will abide.
For every stitch, a story told,
In the enchanted realm, our hearts behold.

Voices Beneath the Dew-Drenched Leaves

In dawn's embrace, the silence breaks,
As whispers weave through ancient oaks.
Voices rise from roots below,
In dew-drenched leaves, the secrets flow.

The faun's soft tune on misty morn,
Unfolds the day, a tale reborn.
Each note, a spell, cast in delight,
Beneath the leaves, in gentle light.

A chorus hums from nature's heart,
Each creature plays a vital part.
From branches high to earth below,
Their voices fuse in sacred glow.

With every raindrop, every sigh,
The forest breathes, the spirits fly.
In unity, their song resounds,
Voices beneath where magic bounds.

So listen close, and you might find,
The stories left that time designed.
In every leaf, in every sigh,
The whispers of the woodlands lie.

The Silver Gleam of Gossamer Elves

In the heart of night, when shadows gleam,
Five tiny sprites, a silver dream.
With wings like silk, they flit and dart,
Their laughter spills, they never part.

Gossamer threads, they weave with grace,
In moonlit glades, their secret place.
With every turn, the stars align,
As magic flows through every line.

They sprinkle dust on slumber's eyes,
Awake the dreams, the gentle sighs.
In silver pools where reflections gleam,
The elves invite you to their dream.

Through woven paths of starlit trails,
They beckon forth with whispered tales.
In enchanted woods where wonders swell,
The silver gleam, they weave so well.

So take a breath, let worries melt,
In gossamer realms, your heart is felt.
For every twinkling, every beam,
The silver gleam shall weave your dream.

Tresses Touched by Nature's Breath

Beneath the canopy, roots entwine,
Tresses wild, a design divine.
With leaves that dance in the softest air,
Nature's breath flows without a care.

Sunbeams filter through boughs so wide,
Illuminating paths where secrets bide.
Each strand, a story, each twist, a rhyme,
In nature's weave, we lose all time.

As blossoms sway to the gentle breeze,
The world around us begins to ease.
With every gust, the whispers sound,
Of tresses touched by life profound.

In every petal, a secret pressed,
In nature's arms, our souls find rest.
Embrace the wild and let it be,
In tresses touched by nature, free.

So wander forth and find your grace,
Among the trees, in wild embrace.
For every heartbeat, every sigh,
In nature's breath, we learn to fly.

Mystic Braids Under Starry Canopies

In twilight's glow, the whispers weave,
A tapestry of dreams they leave.
With every strand, a tale unfolds,
Of secret skies and starlit gold.

Beneath the arch of ancient trees,
The night air swirls with silent pleas.
As braids entwine with moonlit grace,
A magic stirs in this hidden space.

Echoes of laughter dance on high,
With breezy breath, the spirits sigh.
In knots of truth, the fables lie,
A mystical bond, we can't deny.

Stars twinkle down, a knowing glance,
Inviting hearts to join the dance.
Together spun in nature's art,
These mystic braids will never part.

So as we weave, let worries fade,
In this embrace, our fears are laid.
A celestial map, our hearts will share,
In the mystic braids, we breathe the air.

Light as Air: The Dance of Fae Hair

Upon the breeze, they weave and twirl,
With ribbons bright, the fae girls whirl.
Their laughter sprinkles, soft like rain,
In a world where joy holds no disdain.

With every flick, their hair takes flight,
A shimmering cascade, pure delight.
Glimmers of magic caught in strands,
Enchanting all who grasp their hands.

The moonlight holds a silken thread,
As dreams awaken, and fears are shed.
In twilight's kiss, the fae will sway,
A dance of magic, night and day.

With every turn, they spark the sky,
Like stardust trails that dare to fly.
And in their wake, they leave a charm,
A soothing touch, a gentle balm.

So join the dance, let worries melt,
In a world where love and laughter felt.
Light as air, their spirits gleam,
Together we'll weave a wondrous dream.

A Tangle of Secrets Beneath the Moon

Beneath the moon, in shadows deep,
A tangle brews, where secrets keep.
With softest sighs, the night unfolds,
Whispers of tales the darkness holds.

In gnarled roots, the stories sprawl,
Of distant lands and ancient call.
Threads of fate entwined so tight,
In this embrace of endless night.

A silver glow on hidden paths,
Revealing wonders and loved pasts.
With every breath, a bond we share,
In tangled secrets, love's sweet air.

The stars above, they wink and nod,
As if they know what dreams are trod.
In every shadow, a spark of light,
A dance of truths in moonlit flight.

So trust the night, let worries fade,
As secrets bloom in magic's shade.
Beneath the moon, we find our way,
A tangle of secrets, night and day.

Whimsy in the Canopy's Embrace

In the canopy where laughter plays,
Whimsy dances through the days.
With every leaf that catches light,
A tale unfolds, so pure and bright.

The branches sway, a gentle call,
Inviting dreams, enchanting all.
With colors bold and laughter sweet,
The forest whispers, a rhythmic beat.

Joy spirals up with every sigh,
As fae and sprites flit softly by.
In this embrace of nature's grace,
We find our heart's most sacred place.

The morning dew, a soft caress,
In every moment, time's finesse.
With whimsy wrapped in nature's fold,
A world of magic, bright and bold.

So let us dance beneath the trees,
With open hearts, like playful breeze.
In the canopy, our spirits soar,
In whimsy's hold, we crave for more.

Dewy Petals in the Hair of Fae

In twilight's hush, where secrets dwell,
The fae do weave their whispered spell,
With dewy petals bright and rare,
They crown their heads with gentle care.

Each blossom sings a fragrant tune,
Beneath the watchful silver moon,
Their laughter dances on the breeze,
A melody that bends the trees.

In hidden glades, where shadows play,
The fae creatures come out to sway,
With twinkling eyes like stars at night,
They bloom beneath the pale starlight.

They gather dreams from daisies small,
And paint the world with magic's call,
Their joyful hearts in harmony,
Dance through the air, wild and free.

So when you find a petal's trace,
Remember well their wondrous grace,
In every drop of dew that gleams,
There lies the heart of all your dreams.

Shadows that Dance in Nature's Hair

In emerald hues beneath the trees,
The shadows twist with playful ease,
They follow whispers of the night,
As fireflies blink with fleeting light.

Each rustling leaf tells tales untold,
Of adventures brave and spirits bold,
In nature's hair, both wild and fair,
The shadows dance without a care.

They twirl with grace, the wind their friend,
In twilight's embrace, where dreams transcend,
With every flicker, laughter's sound,
In glades and groves, their joy is found.

As moonlight paints the world in silver,
The shadows hug the earth and quiver,
They weave their stories, soft and clear,
In nature's breath, they disappear.

So take a moment, breathe it in,
The shadow dance where dreams begin,
In every rustle, in every sigh,
Nature whispers, and shadows fly.

Reflections of the Moonlit Canopy

Beneath the boughs of ancient trees,
The moonlight spills like silver seas,
It kisses leaves with gentle grace,
And paints the night with soft embrace.

In every glimmer, dreams arise,
A symphony beneath the skies,
With soft cascades of shimmering light,
The canopy blooms in endless night.

Echoes of whispers, softly tread,
As woodland creatures make their bed,
They bask beneath the lunar glow,
In harmony, their secrets flow.

The stars align in quiet cheer,
As night unfolds, they draw us near,
Inviting hearts to join the dance,
In moonlit dreams, we dare to prance.

As dawn approaches, shadows blend,
The magic lingers, never ends,
In every rustle, every sigh,
Reflections of the night stand by.

The Glimmer of Magic in Each Strand

In the warmth of day, where sunlight weaves,
The magic shimmers in tangled leaves,
Each strand of light, a story spun,
Of journeys taken, battles won.

With every breeze, enchantments sway,
In nature's grip, they dance and play,
A fleeting glimpse of wonder's grace,
In every corner, in every place.

Through whispered tales of ancient lore,
In glimmers bright, we search for more,
The tapestry of life reveals,
A world where every heart can feel.

So wander forth, and let it be,
That magic thrives in you and me,
In laughter shared, in love's demand,
We find the glimmer, hand in hand.

Embrace the light, let shadows fall,
For in this dance, we heed the call,
With every heartbeat, take a stand,
The magic of life in each strand.

Fae-Fluttered Curls in the Mist

In dawn's soft glow the fae do play,
With curls that dance in light's array.
Mist wraps around, a silken thread,
Where dreams are spun and softly tread.

They flit through shadows, laughs like bells,
While nature whispers ancient spells.
In every flutter, magic weaves,
A tapestry that none believe.

Moonbeams catch their playful schemes,
As every moment fuels our dreams.
A world unseen in twinkling muck,
With fae-fluttered curls that leave us struck.

In silent glades, they rest at last,
While echoes of their laughter past.
Among the petals strewn with dew,
Their gentle tales in silence brew.

So when the mist begins to swell,
Listen closely, hear their spell.
In every leaf, in every sigh,
They linger on, though time slips by.

Mystical Threads that Whisper in the Wind

Through branches high the whispers flow,
A tapestry of tales aglow.
Each thread of silk, a secret kept,
By ancient trees where shadows slept.

They weave their stories, soft and bright,
In starry skies and morning light.
A gentle touch, a breath of breeze,
That dances through the swaying trees.

In twilight's glow, their whispers hum,
A melody of where they're from.
With every gust, they reach our ears,
A symphony that calms our fears.

These threads of magic, spun so fine,
Connect our hearts, like fate's design.
So sit, be still, and close your eyes,
For wisdom waits beneath the skies.

In whispers low, they call our name,
Embrace the wild, feel the same.
For in their grasp, we're never lost,
In mystical threads, our hearts embossed.

Moonlit Braid of Celestial Beauty

Under the moon, a braid is spun,
Of silver light and shadows run.
Each strand a wish, each knot a prayer,
In cosmic depths, our souls lay bare.

The stars entwined in every twist,
In celestial beauty, none can resist.
They whisper softly through the night,
In dreams of wonder, pure delight.

A tapestry of softest glow,
Guiding lost hearts where they must go.
Through realms unseen, on paths unknown,
In moonlit braids, true love is sewn.

Each pulse of light, a secret share,
In darkness deep, we find our care.
With open hearts, we let it shine,
For in this braid, forever's line.

So when the night begins to fall,
Look to the sky, heed the call.
For in the moon, a braid we find,
Celestial beauty intertwined.

Captured Echoes Among the Leaves

In forest deep where secrets lie,
I hear the echoes, soft and shy.
Among the leaves that gently sway,
In whispers of a bygone day.

Each rustling sound, a tale reborn,
Of lovers lost and legends worn.
The branches cradle stories near,
In captured echoes, hearts can hear.

They speak of magic, time, and fate,
Of enchanted realms, they contemplate.
In every word a spark ignites,
As day enfolds into the nights.

So close your eyes and breathe it in,
Their timeless tales, their sweet kinspin.
In every echo, strength and grace,
In whispered love, we find our place.

Among the leaves where shadows play,
The echoes linger, come what may.
In nature's arms, we're never alone,
For captured echoes lead us home.

Tresses Adrift on the Breath of Night

In the stillness where shadows play,
Tresses drift in the moon's gentle sway.
Whispers of dreams like soft-spun gold,
Dance on the breeze, as stories unfold.

Stars twinkle in the dark velvet sky,
As secrets and wishes from soft lips fly.
Each strand a tale of sorrow and cheer,
Woven with magic, whispered so near.

Nights woven with silken threads of time,
Embrace the heart in an ancient rhyme.
Ghostly silhouettes spin in delight,
In tresses adrift on the breath of night.

As the dawn breaks, the colors ignite,
Fading away in the warm morning light.
Yet deep in the corners of dreams, they'll stay,
A tapestry woven, never to fray.

Gossamer Dreams in Faerie Fields

In faerie fields where the flowers bloom,
Gossamer dreams weave away the gloom.
Soft fluttering wings, echoes of glee,
Paint gentle whispers of how it should be.

Mushrooms stand guard in their silvery glow,
Guardians of secrets the soft winds blow.
Children of starlight in laughter abound,
Crisp autumn leaves make a soft, rustling sound.

Through thickets of thorns and wild briar,
The fae weave enchantments that take one higher.
With glimmers of joy that twinkle like dew,
A world of pure wonder beckons anew.

Each night spins a tale of delight unearned,
As hearts intertwined in soft magic yearned.
In faerie fields, where magic is real,
Gossamer dreams in a silken appeal.

When morning arrives with its crystalline light,
These dreams linger on, ephemeral flight.
Echoing laughter, a flutter once lost,
In faerie fields, no soul ever cost.

The Veil of Night's Enchantment

Under the cloak of the silvered night,
A veil of enchantment shimmers in light.
Soft shadows cast by the stars above,
Whispering secrets of magic and love.

Moonbeams dance on the dew-kissed ground,
Echoing laughter as dreams swirl around.
With each fluttering heart, the cosmos sighs,
Dancing with wonders that never despise.

In the still of the night, all fears take flight,
As creatures emerge with eyes shining bright.
Spells woven softly with delicate threads,
To shroud the world where the magic spreads.

As dawn approaches, the shadows retreat,
But echoes of night weave a soft, warm beat.
In the heart of the dreamers, the magic will stay,
A veil of enchantment that guides their way.

Colorful Flourishes of the Fae

In gardens adorned with a painter's hand,
Colorful flourishes across the land.
Each petal a note in a grand melody,
Sung by the fae in their jubilee.

A riot of hues that glisten and gleam,
Twisting in joy, a whimsical dream.
From blossoms that shimmer under the sun,
To twilight's embrace where the dance has begun.

Threads of laughter on breezes do sail,
While echoes of magic their visions unveil.
With every soft whisper and fluttering cheer,
The colors of faeries banish all fear.

As twilight descends, the hues come alive,
In magical realm where the kind spirits thrive.
Bathed in starlight, they weave and entwine,
Colorful flourishes in rhythm divine.

Though morning will call with its gentle bright touch,
The love of the fae lingers ever so much.
In colors that dance along nature's green,
Colorful flourishes in twilight's sheen.

Lullabies of the Glimmering Foliage

In the hush of night, leaves gently sway,
Soft whispers of magic dance in the gray.
Moonbeams weave tales of the forest so deep,
Nurtured by dreams, the weary ones sleep.

Crickets provide a symphonic refrain,
As shadows enchant the enchanted terrain.
A lullaby sung from the heart of the wood,
Every soft note stitching dreams where they stood.

Glimmering foliage drapes in the light,
Embracing the stars, bidding day farewell night.
While whispers of breeze cradle sighs in the air,
A promise of magic, beyond all compare.

Night birds echo songs to the end of the glen,
Reminders of moments both lost and found then.
With every heartbeat, the forest responds,
To lull the lost souls through symphonic bonds.

In slumber, they drift on the gossamer beams,
Untangling whispers of half-forgotten dreams.
So rest, little ones, let the world fade away,
For the glimmering foliage holds twilight at bay.

The Serenade of Spectral Strands

In the twilight's glow, shadows take flight,
Spectral strands shimmer in the dimming light.
A tapestry woven with whispers so bold,
Stories of ages, in silence, unfold.

Elusive figures move through the trees,
Sighs of the ancients carried on the breeze.
They serenade softly, their voices so clear,
Entwining with secrets that only they hear.

Silvered mist curls like delicate lace,
Enveloping memories time cannot erase.
As echoes of laughter cling to the night,
Filling the air with ethereal light.

Each flickering star tells a tale of old,
Of love lost and found, of hearts brave and bold.
In the depths of the night, their stories resound,
A serenade whispered where enchantment is found.

So wander, brave souls, through the shimmer and glow,
Where spectral strands weave a tapestry slow.
Let the magic embrace you, in dreams take your stand,
Lost in the song of the spectral strand.

Dew-Kissed Waves of Woodland

Morning light drapes over the waking land,
Dew-kissed waves ripple, as nature's hand.
Over mossy carpets where soft shadows play,
Woodland secrets rise with the dawn's gentle sway.

The whispers of leaves in the cool morning air,
Call forth the creatures, both timid and rare.
A symphony stirs as the sun breaks the dawn,
Enchanted by wonders, as dreams carry on.

Gentle the breezes that flutter and tease,
With scents of the earth weaving art from the trees.
In nooks of the forest, soft stories reside,
The dew-kissed waves tend to dreams held inside.

A dance of gold shadows, pure magic it seems,
Awakens the heart to the sweet pulse of dreams.
Each droplet a token, reflecting the skies,
Guiding the wanderer, a soul that aspires.

So linger in moments, let time gently flow,
For the woodland whispers, with secrets to show.
The dew-kissed waves cradle the dreams of the day,
With each breath of morning, let worries drift away.

Ethereal Coils like Silver Streams

In the depths of the night, where dreams intertwine,
Ethereal coils weave a path so divine.
Like silver streams flowing with whispers of fate,
They carry the hopes of the dreamers' estate.

In twilight's embrace, the coils softly glow,
Guiding wayfarers through shadows below.
A tapestry spun of the stories unspoken,
Binds the hearts ready, where silence is broken.

With each gentle turn, a new tale is spun,
Of souls on their journey, from dusk until sun.
These silver streams shimmer with laughter and tears,
A dance of the ages, transcending the years.

Whispers of longing drift soft on the air,
Flowing between worlds, they invite us to care.
A luminous calling from the heart of the night,
In ethereal coils, find solace and light.

So dive into dreams where the silver streams play,
And bask in the magic that beckons your way.
Let the coils hold your heart as you drift off to sleep,
In the glow of the starlit promises deep.

The Twilight Tangle of Fairy Hair

In twilight's caress, the fairies play,
With strands of starlight spun in a sway.
Their laughter dances on the breeze,
Whispers of magic among the trees.

Each tangle a story, each knot a spell,
Secrets enfolded, stories to tell.
Through glimmers of dusk, their giggles entwine,
In the soft, shimmering glow, they brightly shine.

With every flicker of firefly light,
They weave dreams and wishes, taking flight.
The air, thick with wonder, hums low and sweet,
As the world is wrapped in their laughter's retreat.

Oh, to capture a strand, a glimpse at their lore,
A fleeting connection, just wanting more.
For in every braid lies a truth to behold,
An ancient enchantment in threads spun of gold.

As shadows grow long and the night starts to fade,
The fairies retreat, their secrets well-played.
Yet echoes remain in the hush of the night,
In the twilight tangle, a glimpse of their light.

Silhouette of Whispers in the Wind

A silhouette lingers, whispering soft,
Like secrets untold, they drift and waft.
The sigh of the leaves, a gentle refrain,
Carrying tales from the cool, misty plain.

In shadows and moonlight, whispers entwine,
Tracing the edges of dreams, so divine.
Each fluttering sound, a soft, silent plea,
Echoes of voices, lost in the spree.

Through valleys and hills, the murmurs meander,
A dance of the breezes, a sweet, subtle candor.
With each turn of the wind, a new story begins,
Life's tapestry woven where magic spins.

They speak of the starlight that glimmers above,
Of long-forgotten tales and the warmth of love.
In each fleeting breath, adventure awaits,
In the silhouette's whispers, destiny waits.

So listen, dear heart, to the whispers of night,
Find solace in shadows, in pure, ethereal light.
For in every breeze that caresses your ear,
Lives the soft echo of dreams drawing near.

Secrets of Tresses Under Moonbeams

Beneath moonlit skies, where dreams take their flight,
Lies a realm of enchantment, veiled from the light.
With tendrils of silver and whispers of gold,
Secrets are spun, ancient and bold.

In the thicket of night, where wonders entwine,
Each strand of their hair holds a story divine.
A glimmering promise, a soft, gentle sigh,
The secrets of starlight, forever awry.

Tresses that shimmer like dew on the grass,
Hold the echoes of laughter from moments that pass.
In the weave of their locks, the universe spins,
A tapestry woven with losses and wins.

Underneath the vast canvas, dreams stretch and grow,
Hidden within, the cosmos' soft glow.
Each twist and each turn tells a tale anew,
Of wishes made real and hopes breaking through.

The night whispers softly, 'Come closer, and see,'
For within each lock lies the key to be free.
With every brushstroke, a promise to keep,
In the cradle of slumber, where secrets still sleep.

A Flicker of Delicate Shades

In a hush of twilight, where colors ignite,
A flicker of shades dances, tender and bright.
Soft pastels linger, like whispers of spring,
Each hue a reminder of joy they can bring.

From blush of the dawn to the deep shades of dusk,
In a world of transitions, the colors must trust.
They blend and they mingle, creating a song,
Harmonies vibrant, where all shades belong.

With every soft stroke of the artist's kind hand,
A flicker of magic takes shape on the land.
From lavender skies to the emerald leaves,
Delicate shades weave the art that believes.

In the heart of the moment, these colors will sway,
Transforming the ordinary, brightening the gray.
With flickers of wonder, both gentle and bold,
The beauty of life in these shades unfolds.

So cherish each flicker, each color, each hue,
For in their soft dance lies a world bold yet true.
A canvas of life, where dreams can cascade,
In the flicker of delicate shades, magic is made.

Whispers of Enchanted Tresses

In shadowed glades where secrets play,
The whispers curl in twilight's sway,
Each strand a tale, a breath of fate,
Where magic stirs, and dreams await.

Beneath the boughs of whispered lore,
The tresses dance, a silken score,
They twine with stars, embrace the night,
In every twist, a spark of light.

Glimmers of gold, such luster rare,
Entwined with echoes of mystic air,
A tapestry spun of purest glee,
In every wave, the heart's decree.

A gentle breeze, the secret grows,
Tresses weave tales of moonlit prose,
A crown of dreams upon her brow,
Eternal whispers, here and now.

So let the echoes softly grace,
This world of magic, time and space,
For every strand, a promise kept,
In whispers, ancient promises slept.

Gleaming Strands of Myth

In ancient woods where shadows gleam,
The strands of myth entwine a dream,
With every lock, a story spins,
Of battles fought and love that wins.

Gleaming threads of silver light,
Woven carefully through the night,
They shimmer bright with every sigh,
Where legends breathe and sorrows fly.

A maiden's hair, a river's grace,
Reflects the stars in its embrace,
Each strand a bridge to lands unknown,
In every twist, a seed is sown.

With whispers soft as evening's breath,
They carry echoes of a death,
And yet rebirth through time's vast maze,
A tapestry of twilight's haze.

So gather round, and listen well,
To gleaming strands, their lore to tell,
For in each wave, a myth sustains,
A bond eternal, where magic reigns.

Velvet Locks in Twilight

In twilight's hush, the velvet falls,
Soft echo in the ancient halls,
Where locks like shadows gleam and sway,
And dusk enfolds the fading day.

Each tender strand, a touch of night,
Entwined with dreams, the stars alight,
Their softness holds a power deep,
A vision woven, secrets keep.

With every wave, the twilight sighs,
As velvet whispers touch the skies,
They gleam like embers in the dark,
A flickering flame, an ancient spark.

A symphony of softest hues,
Where secrets dance in evening's muse,
Velvet locks that speak in rhymes,
Of days long past and hidden times.

So let the velvet grace unfold,
A tale of magic, softly told,
In twilight's arms, forever bound,
Where whispers of the night are found.

Moonlit Curls of the Otherworld

In moon's embrace, the curls entwine,
A dance of fate, a twist of time,
Each spiral gleaming, softly spun,
A journey beckons, just begun.

Through silver skies, the whispers flow,
As ancient secrets start to glow,
In curls that breathe the night's allure,
A tapestry of dreams, so pure.

They shimmer bright with every light,
Reflecting tales of day and night,
The otherworld, a beckoning call,
Where magic lingers, touching all.

So let the moonlit curls expand,
A cosmic bridge across the land,
For in each loop, a portal wakes,
To realms unseen, as silence breaks.

In every twirl, a truth revealed,
A bond of worlds, forever sealed,
The otherworld through curls shall gleam,
Awake the heart, and spark a dream.

A Wisp of Wonder in the Evening Glow

The sun sinks low in the embrace of night,
Where shadows dance in soft, golden light.
Whispers of magic drift through the air,
A wisp of wonder, both gentle and rare.

Flickering fireflies twinkle like stars,
In gardens where dreams weave their mystic bars.
The world holds its breath, a secret it keeps,
As twilight descends and the silence deepens.

In the hush of dusk, hearts begin to roam,
Seeking the comfort, the light of home.
Every corner glimmers with stories untold,
In the evening glow, a magic unfolds.

The trees sway softly, a lullaby sung,
Where memories linger and hopes are sprung.
With every heartbeat, time seems to stall,
A wisp of wonder, embracing us all.

As stars twinkle shyly, they join in the play,
Guiding our dreams on this twilight's ballet.
Every moment expansive, the world's aglow,
In the gentle embrace of the evening's flow.

Dreamlike Spirals in Secret Gardens

In gardens hidden from the light of day,
Dreamlike spirals beckon us to stay.
Where petals whisper secrets in the breeze,
And time dances lightly among the trees.

The colors swirl like a painter's brush,
Each blossom unfolds, igniting a hush.
A symphony hums in this tranquil space,
As we wander through nature's warm embrace.

Beneath the boughs, the world feels anew,
In secret corners, where magic is brewed.
With every step, possibilities soar,
As adventure awaits behind every door.

The moon peeks softly through a leafy veil,
Guiding our footsteps on this mystic trail.
With laughter and whispers, we share delight,
In dreamlike spirals, embraced by the night.

In the heart of the garden, a fountain sings,
Of wishes and hopes that the night gently brings.
We gather our dreams, like stars in the air,
In secret gardens, where all is laid bare.

Tresses Beneath a Spiral of Stars

Tresses of silver weave through the night,
Beneath a canopy of stars, so bright.
In the stillness, whispers of the past,
Echo like memories, frail yet vast.

With every twinkle, a tale comes alive,
Of lovers and dreamers, who dared to strive.
In this tapestry spun from hope's gentle hand,
We find our reflections across the land.

The moon's soft gaze casts a silken glow,
Embracing the secrets that only we know.
Under the spiral of stars, we belong,
In a world of enchantment, where hearts are strong.

As shadows long dance to a silent tune,
We weave our wishes beneath the blue moon.
Each heartbeat a rhythm, each sigh a part,
Of stories entwined in the threads of the heart.

Time drifts like clouds, yet we stand so still,
In the embrace of night, our dreams to fulfill.
With tresses alight, and spirits set free,
We twirl through the cosmos, just you and me.

The Enchantment of the Greener Lands

In the greener lands, where magic appears,
Nature paints beauty through laughter and tears.
With valleys that cradle the sun's warm glow,
And rivers that dance with a shimmering flow.

Spirits of woodland rejoice in delight,
As shadows unfurl under soft, starlit night.
Each leaf a whisper, each breeze a song,
In the heart of the forest, where we all belong.

The flowers awake to the dawn's gentle kiss,
In vibrant hues, we find moments of bliss.
The wind carries tales from the mountains so grand,
Of journeys and dreams in these enchanting lands.

As twilight descends, the world holds its breath,
In silence profound, for life, and for death.
But fear not, dear friend, for the magic is near,
In the greener lands, let your heart steer clear.

So wander with me, where the wildflowers bloom,
In the enchantment that scatters away gloom.
For here in this haven, life sparkles and gleams,
In the greener lands, we nurture our dreams.

www.ingramcontent.com/pod-product-compliance
Ingram Content Group UK Ltd.
Pitfield, Milton Keynes, MK11 3LW, UK
UKHW021505280125
4335UKWH00035B/700